Learning the Business Marketing Way

A Simplified Way to Attract New Customers, make them Committed, Stand Out in a Busy Market, and Achieve Success

By

Francis A. Wiles

Learning the Business Marketing Way

Copyright

Disclaimer

The content in this book is meant only for general informative purposes. Although the author has taken every precaution to ensure that the material is correct and current, there are no express or implied guarantees or warranties of any kind regarding the availability, accuracy, appropriateness, completeness, or reliability of the information provided herein. You assume all risks associated with relying on such material.

Any loss or harm resulting from using the material in this book is not the author's responsibility. For situation-specific counsel, it is recommended that you speak with a certified specialist.

The opinions and viewpoints conveyed in this book belong to the author and may not necessarily represent the official stance or policies of any organizations referenced.

About the Author

Francis A. Wiles is a seasoned business professional who has left an everlasting imprint across multiple industries. He has become a beacon of empowerment for businesses trying to thrive rather than just survive. Francis Aguides entrepreneurs with a passion for turning obstacles into possibilities.

From navigating complex business landscapes to promoting innovation, Francis has earned a reputation for smart leadership. Through his endeavors, he has consistently shown an exceptional capacity to condense complexity into practical strategies, enabling organizations to not only navigate but thrive in the face of change.

This book, Learning the Business Way, is the result of Wiles's depth of expertise and dedication to fostering success. Dive into these pages for practical ideas, tried-and-true tactics, and the assistance you need to enhance your business and stand out in today's competitive landscape. Join Wiles on this transforming journey to business excellence.

INTRODUCTION

The significance of a simplified marketing plan

In society at the moment's society, especially in recent times, it's unsolvable to enjoy a little or large- scale business or work for an association without understanding the value of marketing. Marketing is an important aspect to consider anyhow of the size of a business, whether it's new or established. A business may not be suitable to operate for long if it doesn't have a successful marketing plan in place.

Marketing plans are documents that experts produce to outline marketing enterprise and the conditioning needed to put recommended tactics into action. Marketing plans are vital because they outline the exact way that platoon members want to take in order to reach out to target guests, raise brand mindfulness, and induce income.

A marketing plan is necessary for a variety of reasons, but then are four main bones:

1. Strategic Guidance: A marketing plan serves as a road chart for your company's marketing enterprise. It outlines your pretensions, target followership, and styles, aiding you in staying on track and working toward your pretensions.

2. Resource Allocation: It aids in the effective allocation of coffers. You can budget for marketing sweats, emplace people, time, and coffers where they're most productive, and avoid gratuitous spending if you have a plan in place

3. Stability and Cohesion: A well- planned marketing strategy ensures that your messaging and imprinting remain harmonious across all media. This thickness reinforces your brand's identity and fosters trust among your target followership.

4. Measurable issues: Performance criteria and targets are constantly included in a marketing plan. This allows you to track your progress and estimate the effectiveness of your marketing juggernauts, making it easier to modify and enhance your strategy.

A marketing plan, in substance, is a necessary tool for remaining organized, effective, and effective in your marketing sweats. A marketing plan's success is also determined by how simple the plans are to execute.

A simple marketing strategy is useful for colorful reasons

1. Details: It gives a terse and clear picture of your marketing approach. This simplicity ensures that your platoon and stakeholders understand and can fluently follow the plan.

2. Focus: A straightforward strategy lets you concentrate on the most pivotal objects and styles. It stops you from being overwhelmed with unwanted details and diversions.

3. Completion: Simplicity frequently leads to superior execution. When your marketing strategy is simple to understand, your team is more likely to implement it effectively and consistently.

4. Aptitude for Change: Simple plans are easier to adapt to changing conditions. This agility is critical in the fast-paced world of marketing, where the ability to pivot rapidly can provide a considerable advantage.

5. Conversation: A concise plan is easier to communicate to your staff, stakeholders, and investors. Everyone can be on the same page, which is vital for successful collaboration.

Resource Efficient A basic strategy allows you to efficiently deploy resources since you can easily determine where your time, budget, and effort are most needed. A basic marketing plan is all about clarity, concentration, and efficiency. It enables you to reach your marketing objectives without adding excessive complication.

CHAPTER 1: Taking the First Step and Don't Get it Mixed Up

A marketing plan is one of the most significant papers in a company's long- term success. When done rightly, it's a road chart that examines the business terrain, troubles and possibilities in the sector, and implements a marketing strategy to reach commercial pretensions. This isn't the same as a standard business strategy. A marketing plan is more concerned with strategy, whereas a business plan is more concerned with finances. Likewise, a business plan is frequently used to help associations raise backing, but a marketing plan tries to give direction for a company and is a vital element of a business plan.

The request exploration you conduct will impact the opinions you make when developing your marketing plan. Who are your guests? Will you target individualities or businesses? Which is better, direct or noncommercial? How does your product meet their demands and requirements? You will need to understand their pretensions and requirements, as well as their studies and beliefs, communication preferences, price comfort, and how your product"checks the boxes"for them.

A marketing plan is a strategic roadmap used by enterprises to organize, apply, and track their marketing strategy over a specific time period. Marketing plans might comprise multitudinous marketing tactics for colorful marketing brigades throughout the establishment, all of which are working toward the same business pretensions. A marketing plan builds a unified roadmap for where your marketing sweats should take your establishment grounded on your overall marketing strategy. A marketing plan's ideal is to have a defined path to follow in order to acquire new guests, enhance connections with present guests and guests, boost deals, ameliorate retention, and raise brand mindfulness.

It's critical to understand that marketing strategies can and will evolve. Indeed if your markcting pretensions remain the same, it's usual to make changes to your marketing strategy grounded on any changes in the marketing conditions that was when the plan was first developed. generally, completing request exploration is the original stage in developing a marketing plan. This entails gathering vital data for educated decision- making by probing your target followership, rivals, and assiduity trends.

clearly! When developing a marketing strategy, the first stage is to request exploration. Then is a more in- depth breakdown of what this entails .

1. Define Your Ideal guests: Begin by defining your ideal guests. Who exactly are they? What are their characteristics, interests, and conditions? Understanding your target followership allows you to direct your marketing sweats to the correct people.

2. Contender Evaluation: Probe your competition. What are their advantages and disadvantages? How do they promote their goods or services? This exploration might help you in relating possibilities to separate your company.

3. Request Developments: Keep an eye on current assiduity trends and developments. Technological improvements, changes in client geste , and rising request openings are exemplifications of this.

4. SWOT Analysis: Conduct a geek analysis to estimate your own company. Determine your advantages, disadvantages, openings, and pitfalls. This tone- evaluation is critical for knowing your internal capabilities as well as external problems.

5. Develop Marketing objects: Grounded on your findings, develop clear and specific marketing objects. These should be measurable and applicable to your overall business pretensions.

6. Budget Planning: Determine how important plutocrat you are willing to spend on marketing. Your budget will have an impact on the styles and approaches you can employ.

Conducting thorough request exploration provides significant perceptivity that informs the rest of your marketing plan, similar as which marketing channels to use, what messaging connects with your target demographic, and how to effectively place your particulars or services in the request. This exploration- grounded approach improves the chances of a successful marketing strategy.

Selecting a Target Followership

The customer controls the purchasing process, and marketers must make focused, acclimatized gests, for guests if they want to stand out among an ocean of brands and announcements. Your target followership is the exact set of consumers who are most likely to want your product or service, and therefore the bones who should see your advertising sweats. Age, gender, wealth, position, interests, and a variety of other criteria can all impact the target followership. The target followership is a defined set of people. These individualities may be men, women, youths, or children. They generally have a common interest, similar to reading, exercising, or playing soccer. Advertisers might use personas to explore applicable magazine titles or assiduity publications.

What Are the Different Types of Target Cult?

Target cult can be further subdivided into intent, position, interests, and other factors. Let's look at some exemplifications of how you can member your target followership:

Separate groups according to their different interests, similar as pursuits and entertainment choices:
This can help you in creating data- driven, largely acclimatized dispatches that allows you to connect with your followership in meaningful ways and induce brand fidelity.

Buying Intention: Define groups of people who are seeking a specific product, similar to a new TV or auto. This will help you in understanding your followership's pain spots, allowing you to induce targeted messaging that meets their requirements.

Mores: Mores are groups of people who partake in a common experience, similar as music stripes or fandoms in entertainment. You can more grasp who you are trying to connect with if you understand some of your target followership's reasons.

The Distinction Between a Target followership and a Target Market

A target request is a group of consumers to whom a pot intends to vend or reach through marketing operations. A target followership is the group or part of a target request to which advertising is given. As a result, the target followership becomes a more technical subset of a target request. To return to the running shoe illustration, let's imagine your target request is lengthy runners, but you are offering a special at your Boston position. The target followership for a trade announcement would be prospective Boston Marathon runners, not all marathon runners. Because it's a specified subset of the largest request group, target followership and target request are constantly used interchangeably. Still, target requests aren't always synonymous with target followership.

Understanding Your Target followership's places

Going beyond knowing demographic information to understand what part they play in the road to buy is a critical step in understanding your target followership. Flash back, the better you understand your target request, the more efficiently you can epitomize your marketing sweats to reach and engage them. It's a nonstop process that demands revision as your company and request evolve.

Formulating your message

Your target followership may be niche or wide depending on what yousell.However, for illustration, your target followership would be different because men, If you were a shoe seller. On the other side, perhaps you specialize in high- performance handling shoes. also your target followership would be more specific- elite athletes progressed 20 to 40 who have expressed an interest in running or have completed a marathon. In either case, it's critical to define and classify your target demographic in order to identify the creative messaging that will reverberate with them and the channels they prefer.

There will really be consumers that fall within your target demographic but don't respond to messaging. Try to be unequivocal about who your target followership is and who it isn't. Is your demographic lady, or ladies aged 20 to 40? Knowing this can help your brigades from wasting plutocrat on announcement parts that won't give results.

Following these way will surely simplify the process of developing a marketing communication after exploration

1. Understand your followership Understand who you are aiming for.

2. Establish pretensions. Decide what you want to negotiate.

3. Emphasize your distinctness Explain why your product or service is remarkable.

4. Craft a conclusive communication that's both clear and charming.

5. select the applicable channels Use platforms that your target followership uses.

6. Maintain brand thickness.

7. trial and ameliorate by testing and adjusting.

8. Track results Keep track of what works and what doesn't.

CHAPTER 2: Furnishing an Exceptional Service

Meeting guests' prospects is the key to furnishing effective client service. furnishing excellent client service entails doing so all and every time a consumer connections you. What comes to mind when you think of your stylish client service experience? A positive client experience can alter how guests see a company. It can also foster fidelity. client satisfaction entails continually exceeding guests' prospects. Great client service is rapid-fire, simple, personalized, and compassionate. Companies that give exceptional client service take the time to understand their specific consumer base's requirements.

10 Strategies to Give Excellent Client Service

It's one thing to strive for excellent client service. Still, unless your challengers give poor client service, you'll need to go over and beyond to distinguish out. Likewise, customer demands are always adding . For numerous businesses, good client service is inadequate. Then is how to elevate your client service from acceptable to exceptional.

- Channel preference
- Empathy
- client- centricity
- visionary backing
- Personalization
- Speed
- tone- service

- Agents with authority
- Collaboration
- dexterity

1. Serve your customers through the style they prefer

Still, you may be inclined to"take that discussion offline"so it doesn't come public, If a client tweets a complaint. Still, it isn't always that simple. maybe they have formerly tried calling your risk-free number and encountered a lengthy delay. Maybe they simply prefer social media for customer service. People choose channels grounded on how snappily they need a result and the complexity of their situation. guests want to communicate with you through the same channels they use to communicate with their musketeers and family. As a result, being suitable to help a client via their favored support channel is one of the finest ways to give excellent client service. Guests want to communicate with you through the same channels they use to communicate with their musketeers and family. Your agents must be suitable to address questions via phone, dispatch, texting, live converse, social media, and other channels. It helps if your system can keep track of everything and allow agents to easily switch between communication channels. For example, assume a consumer begins using live chat but the problem gets too complex to resolve through chat. In that case, you want your agents to be able to quickly switch to a phone conversation.

2. Have compassion

To create a fantastic experience, you must be able to relate to your customers. That begins with empathy, which means putting the client at the center of everything you do and being inspired to serve them—not seeing them as a bother to deal with, but as the hero of your tale. It's an important customer service skill.

3. Customers should be at the core of your orbit

Customer-centric businesses are on the increase, and they are looking for people that are passionate about providing a really exceptional customer experience. It's a successful strategy: Companies with a truly customer-centric culture are 60% more profitable than those without. Customer centricity is a corporate approach that places the customer at the center of all decisions. And it entails more than just providing exceptional customer service (though that is essential). Companies that have a customer-centric culture are 60% more profitable than those that do not. Businesses that wish to be customer-centric must commit to prioritizing people.

Being customer-centric also entails hiring with the customer in mind—employees should perceive the client as the star of the tale, rather than a bother, or problem to be solved. True customer-focused firms collect consumer feedback across all channels and disseminate it across the organization to assist influence business choices. The experience of your customer is equally as crucial (if not more so) as the goods or service you're selling them. Even if your product is excellent, a poor user experience will cause you to lose clients to competition.

4. Be proactive in your assistance

When things don't go as planned, your customer may let you know. And now one problem has become two: resolving the initial issue and attempting to convert an upset client into a pleased one. Excellent customer service frequently entails anticipating your customers' wants before they ever inform you. Proactive customer service occurs when a company takes the initiative to assist a client before the customer approaches them for assistance. It entails attempting to remedy issues as soon as they arise. There are numerous advantages to providing proactive customer service. You can frequently prevent problems from occurring. Instead than waiting for a consumer complaint, you're helping them right now. This saves your customer service staff time and ensures that your customers are satisfied. An agent can recommend things in real-time if you can use client data to learn about their interests. This type of 1:1 care can lead to increased client loyalty and upsell opportunities.

5. Make the experience your own

According to the Zendesk Customer Experience Trends Report, 67% of customers are willing to pay more for an excellent experience. To make a connection, you must use data to tailor the consumer experience. The truth is that most customers now demand a highly personalized experience: they want a company to know who they are, what they've previously purchased, and even their preferences. They also expect you to remember everything because they don't want to repeat themselves. The vast majority of clients are willing to spend more for an exceptional experience. Your clients, in fact, already expect highly individualized service. While consumers are typically hesitant to reveal personal information, according to Accenture research, 83 percent of purchasers are eager to give companies their data if they believe it will lead to more customisation.Of course, you must proceed with caution—protecting consumer data is a major priority. You will lose your customer's trust if you release their data without their specific consent or use it in ways they did not expect. And once damaged, it is difficult for brands to recover trust.

6. Provide prompt client service

Customers have high expectations: they expect you to reply swiftly. Millennials and Generation Z, in particular, prefer outlets that allow for immediate answers, such as:

- Social networking sites

- In-app communication
- Apps for social messaging

It's no surprise that older generations prefer more traditional channels such as phone, email, and in-store encounters. However, respondents' patience for response times is dwindling: 51% want a response in less than five minutes on the phone, and 28% expect the same on live chat. Exceeding expectations entails staying ahead of the competition. That may mean generating an automatic answer for an SMS or email that says, "We got your question, and we're looking into it."It could also mean rapidly returning a call from a client who leaves a message. It's already terrible service if they have to call you twice.

7. Make it simple for customers to assist themselves

Customers do not always want to seek assistance. Sometimes providing exceptional customer service entails allowing individuals to help themselves. Sixty-nine percent of customers prefer to handle as many problems on their own as feasible, and 63 percent always or almost always begin with a search on a company's website. Sometimes providing exceptional customer service entails allowing individuals to help themselves. However, there is a significant gap—many businesses are failing to capitalize on this opportunity. Only one-third of businesses provide a knowledge base or community forum, and less than one-third provide social messaging, chatbots, or in-app messaging. You will ease pressure on your support crew and create happy customers if you develop an easy way for customers to self-help.

8. Provide agents with tools to help them work more efficiently

A good consumer experience and a good employee experience are intimately intertwined, like peanut butter and jelly. According to a Forrester survey, organizations with the most engaged staff had 81 percent higher customer satisfaction, half the turnover of their counterparts, and a decisive competitive edge. Supporting your support team entails providing them with the tools and processes they require to accomplish their tasks effectively. According to our CX Trends Report, higher-performing teams are implementing structural changes to workflows to better meet the demands of their employees.

9. Allow agents to collaborate

Resolving customer concerns frequently necessitates collaboration among agents and other departments, and customers expect firms to collaborate on their behalf. According to our research, 31 percent more agents stated they require technologies that allow them to collaborate across teams internally this year than last. Agents can collaborate both inside and outside the CX organization using platforms like Slack and Zoom in their office.

10. Improve by utilizing your analytics

Support teams want analytics software that provides immediate access to customer information across channels in one place in order to keep up with customer needs. This enables them to be nimble since they can focus on comprehending and reacting to data rather than simply recording it. According to our Trends Report, 40 percent of managers do not have the necessary analytics tools to monitor success for remote teams. Support executives can take action on what's happening right now and understand prior trends thanks to real-time and historical data incorporated into their CX system. They can identify opportunities for team development and understand how clients connect with them in order to improve the entire experience.

How crucial is excellent customer service?

Customer service is a critical difference in the perspective of both customers and businesses. After just one terrible customer service experience, 61 percent of customers would defect to a competitor. Make it two bad experiences, and 76 percent of clients will go.

This increases the pressure on firms to provide excellent customer service. However, it also means that businesses have an opportunity to drive development and reduce churn by providing excellent customer service. For example, 74% of customers say they will forgive a corporation for a mistake if they receive exceptional service.

Creating an Excellent Product

An amazing product is one that exceeds client expectations in terms of quality and performance. It distinguishes itself in its category due to its innovative features, dependability, and longevity, and it frequently gives outstanding value for its price. Outstanding items are held in high regard by users and frequently earn favorable feedback and recommendations.

Creating a great product often entails the following important elements:

1. Clear Purpose: The product should have a clear purpose and answer a specific market problem or demand.

2. User-Centered Design: Focus on the end-user experience by designing the product with usability, accessibility, and aesthetics in mind.

3. High Quality: Make certain that the product meets or exceeds industry standards for quality, performance, and dependability.

4. Incorporate distinctive features or technology that distinguish the product from competition.

5. Market Fit: Understand your target market and match your offering to their needs and tastcs.

6. Scalability refers to the ability of a product to adapt to changing market conditions and demands.

7. Effective Marketing: Create a solid marketing strategy to effectively promote the product and reach potential buyers.

8. Customer Service: Provide great customer service to address user issues and feedback as soon as possible.

9. Pricing Strategy: Provide a pricing strategy that is in line with the product's value proposition and market competition.

10. Continuous Improvement: Update and improve the product on a regular basis depending on customer feedback and changing market conditions.

An exceptional product not only achieves these standards, but also exceeds client expectations, making a positive effect and providing long-term value.

11. Reliability: Ensure that the product functions consistently and with minimal downtime or faults, hence fostering user trust.

12. Implement stringent security measures to secure user data and ensure the product's integrity.

13. Consider environmental and social consequences when developing a product with a low ecological footprint and beneficial society benefits.

14. Cross-Platform Compatibility: Make the product available on multiple devices and platforms in order to reach a larger audience.

15. **Ease of Integration**: Allow the product to integrate effortlessly with other systems and software, increasing its utility.

16. Establish procedures for collecting and analyzing user feedback for continual development.

17. **Agile Development**: Adopt agile approaches to adapt to changing market conditions and efficiently iterate on the product.

18. Risk management entails identifying and mitigating any hazards to the product's success or safety.

19. **Strong Team:** Put together a talented, collaborative team that is enthusiastic about the product's success.

20. Ethical Considerations: Maintain ethical principles and ideals throughout the development process to build trust and reputation.

21. **Intellectual Property:** Use patents, copyrights, or trademarks to protect the product's intellectual property.

22. **Data Analytics:** Use data analytics to create data-driven decisions, improve user experiences, and add new features to your products.

23. **User Education:** Provide materials and support to help users realize the full potential of the product.

Creating an exceptional product is a complicated process that requires careful planning, a thorough understanding of the market and users, and a dedication to ongoing development. It necessitates a comprehensive approach to product development and management.

Shaping your Brand's Personality and Character

It is critical to distinguish between personality and character. Personality refers to value judgments made about a person's morality or ethical behavior, whereas character is the unique way each individual thinks, acts, and feels throughout life. Your brand's personality begins with a detailed examination of your company's key beliefs. Respect, honesty, passion, empowerment, humility, empathy, creativity, and fun are some terms that describe these principles. Concentrate on a few values that will set the tone for your own brand personality.

Brand Personality vs. Brand Character

It is critical to distinguish between a brand character and a brand personality. A brand character is a person you develop to represent your company. A brand personality, on the other hand, is the overall tone and feel of your brand. Your brand character should express the personality of your brand in its own unique way. They should share your brand's values and attributes while also having their own individual personality. Certain qualities should be present in your brand persona when designing it. These characteristics will be unique to your organization, however some examples are:

- **Friendliness:** Your brand character should be someone with whom people desire to interact. They should have confidence in their ability to provide correct information.

- **Expertise**: Your brand's persona should be an authority in their sector. They should be someone to whom people may turn for counsel and direction.

- **Enthusiasm**: Your brand's personality should be ecstatic about your products or services. They should be enthusiastic and enthusiastic in their contacts with customers.

These are just a few characteristics that your brand character could have. It is critical to select attributes that are significant to your organization and those you want people to identify with your brand.

Creating a Brand Persona for Your Company

Developing a brand personality can be a fun and gratifying process. It helps you to consider what distinguishes your brand and what personality you want it to have. It's also a terrific method to involve your team in the branding process.

If you don't know where to begin, there are a few important questions you can ask yourself to help determine your brand's personality.

- What does my brand represent?
- What is the personality of my brand?
- What are the essential values of my brand?
- What do I want my customers to feel when they interact with my brand?

Answering these questions will help you better understand the type of personality you should be developing for your brand.

1. Choose the values that will define your brand's personality

After you've answered these questions, you'll need to pick what values and characteristics you want your character to represent. These should be founded on the mission and brand identity of your organization. After you've settled on them, you may begin thinking about what type of personality will best reflect your company.

2. Create a personality for your brand

Once you've defined your brand's personality, you can consider how you want to bring them to life. To help portray your brand's personality, you can utilize graphics, animations, or even photographs. What matters is that they are visually appealing and easily identifiable.

3. Implement your brand's personality

All of your marketing and advertising materials should reflect your brand's personality. They should be prominently displayed on your website, social media pages, and printed materials. Make sure that everyone on your team understands your brand's personality so that they can deploy it consistently across all platforms.

Advantages of Brand Character

Creating a brand personality has numerous advantages for your firm. You'll be able to give potential customers a face to associate with your firm. Other benefits of brand personalities include:

1. Assisting in emotional development: Assisting in the development of an emotional connection with your audience. When your character embarks on a trip, your emotionally committed audience joins them.

2. Increasing the relatability of your brand: Your target audience may see themselves or their problems in your brand's personality. Certainly, here are some more specific advantages of employing a brand character:

3. Increased Engagement: A charming and relatable brand character can increase audience engagement since consumers are more likely to interact with material featuring a character with whom they identify.

4. Values Mascot: Your brand mascot can embody your business's core values and principles, reinforcing the idea that your company stands for something valuable.

5. Cultural Relevance: A well-designed character may be adapted to many cultural situations, allowing your business to connect with a wide range of people.

6. Long-Term Brand Building: A brand character can become an enduring symbol connected with your company over time, helping to create and recognize your brand over time. Characters can serve as the central figure in several sorts of content, such as videos, blogs, and social media postings, making content development more unified and efficient.

7. Easier Communication: By using a character as a visual aid, complex concepts or features can be simplified and communicated more effectively.

8. Brand Extensions: Using the character's existing reputation, brand extensions can be used to launch additional product lines or services.

9. Customer Loyalty: When people connect with a brand character, they are more likely to become loyal customers and brand supporters.

10. Brand memory: A memorable character helps boost brand memory, ensuring that people consider your brand first while looking for relevant items or services.

11. Positive Associations: A well-liked persona can impact purchasing decisions and client perceptions by creating positive associations with your brand.

12. Versatility in Storytelling: Characters may be employed to create multiple stories and adapt to diverse themes and marketing campaigns, giving you more freedom in your messaging.

13. Brand Characters Can Evolve and Adapt to Changing trends and consumer preferences, ensuring your brand remains relevant.

14. Iconic Status: In some situations, brand figures can become cultural icons, transcending their initial commercial function.

Remember that a brand character's effectiveness is determined by how well it matches with your brand's objectives and resonates with your target audience. Character development and management should be a deliberate and purposeful process. Making it easier for people to recall your brand. They could recall the slogan or design of your character. Making your brand stand out from the crowd. Other organizations may offer a comparable service, but your brand identity is unique to you.

Including a Brand Persona in Your Marketing Strategy

Consider establishing a brand persona if you want to make your brand more recognizable and relatable. You'll be able to emotionally connect with your audience and increase consumer loyalty. Brand personalities, when used effectively, may be a significant asset to your marketing strategy.

Follow these steps to incorporate a brand character into your marketing strategy:

1. Define Your Brand and Audience: Identify your target audience and their preferences, as well as your brand's values, personality, and unique selling factors.

2. Character Development: Create or improve your brand's personality. Define their personality, backstory, and how they relate to the ideals of your brand.

3. Establish Specific Goals: Determine what you want to achieve with your brand's personality. Is it greater brand recognition, engagement, or brand values conveyed?

4. Integrate into Branding: Ensure that your character's visual identity, including colors, typography, and design components, is consistent with your brand's visual identity.

5. Content Strategy: Think about how and where you'll use your character in your content. Website design, social networking, advertising, and packaging are all examples of this.

6. Maintain a consistent presence for your brand's character across all marketing channels to reinforce brand identification.

7. material Creation: Create material featuring your character. This can include videos, blog entries, social media updates, and other forms of media.

8. Storytelling and Narratives: Create narratives and stories that include your character. These stories should be consistent with the messaging and values of your brand.

9. Encourage audience participation with your character through contests, polls, or challenges relating to the character.

10. Evaluate Performance: Use data and analytics to determine how well your brand's personality contributes to your marketing goals. This could include tracking interaction, brand awareness, or sales.

11. Adapt and Evolve: Be prepared to change your persona and how you employ it in response to feedback and shifting marketing trends.

12. Legal Considerations: Make sure you have all of the essential legal rights and protections for your persona, such as trademarks or copyrights.

13. Budgeting: Set aside funds for character development, content creation, and marketing campaigns involving the character.

14. Iteration and testing: A/B test different character-related material and tactics to see what works best for your audience.

15. Cross-Promotion: If appropriate, use your brand character to cross-promote with other brands or influencers.

16. Educate Your staff: Ensure that your marketing staff and everyone else participating in content creation understand the role of the character and how to maintain consistency.

Incorporating a brand character into your marketing strategy can be an effective approach to connect with your target audience and differentiate your brand. To get the most of this method, you must have a clear plan and a thorough grasp of your brand and audience.

CHAPTER 3. Addressing Pricing Sensitivity and sales Channels

Understanding pricing sensitivity is crucial for businesses looking to optimize their pricing strategy and maximize profits. Companies can use price sensitivity analysis to make better judgments about how to price their products and services, assigning the correct price and allowing them to be competitive and improve their revenues. But what exactly is pricing sensitivity, why is it significant, and how can it be calculated? Let us investigate!

What exactly is Pricing Sensitivity?

Pricing sensitivity refers to how the price of a product influences consumers' purchase decisions. This refers to the extent to which the selling of a specific product or service is impacted. In general, it is how demand fluctuates as product prices change. Price elasticity of demand, or the measure of demand change as a function of price change, is a typical way to measure price sensitivity. Price sensitivity varies by consumer; for example, some consumers are willing to pay more when the price of a product rises, while others are not.

1. **The decision-making process of consumers:** Before delving into the price sensitivity process, it is critical to

comprehend consumer behavior during the purchasing decision process:

2. **Recognition**: The buyer recognizes that they are in a "real and preferred state."They want to buy a product, whether through marketing, promotion, or peer pressure.

3. **Information seeking:** The buyer sets out to learn more about what they wish to acquire.

4. **Deliberation:** The client uses the information acquired to choose which options, alternatives, or aspects to examine before advancing. This is when price sensitivity can emerge and you may lose the consumer.

5. **Purchase:** The customer decides and purchases what they want.

6. **Subsequent purchase:** The consumer chooses whether this was what they were looking for, whether it was a good decision, whether they regret it, and whether it is time to return the merchandise or request a refund.

Factors influencing pricing sensitivity

Pricing sensitivity is an important component for firms in making the best decisions and assigning the best rates, thus it is critical to understand the consumer's attitude and behavior. Price sensitivity is affected by the following elements, which are regarded as determinants by consumers when purchasing a product or service.

Cost and quality

Buyers are less price sensitive if the given product is of superior quality or defines their status quo, such as exclusive or luxury goods.

Unique worth

Product differentiation and distinctive features influence consumers' price sensitivity. With unique value products or services, the firm can outperform its competition.

Bottom-line Advantage

If the buyer's utility is high and the product fits his purchasing aim efficiently, he is less bothered about the price.

Fairness

Price discrimination can create a consumer sense of unfair practices. In this case, a minor rise may have a detrimental impact, raising price sensitivity. Expense If the product demands a large investment or has a high cost, the customer is likely to be price sensitive while making a decision.

Inventory

Buyers become more price-conscious when they need to keep their products in stock.

Feeling of impending doom

If there is an immediate need for the product or service, the consumer often disregards the price issue. The case of emergency medical services is one example of this.

Cost-sharing

When someone else pays the price of a product or service on behalf of the consumer, they may not be price sensitive.

Comparison simplicity

Consumers are more price sensitive if they can quickly compare the numerous solutions on the market.

Substitutes as they are perceived

Consumers become highly price sensitive when they can acquire a comparable substitute for a certain product or service at a lower price.

The expense of switching

When switching from one company to another is prohibitively expensive, people prefer to be less price-conscious and stick with a single product or service.

Brand recognition

Brand loyalty in particular brands can be a key influence in determining price sensitivity.

Methods for calculating pricing sensitivity

The goal is to thoroughly understand your target demographic and the people who make purchases. Each of them will view the worth of your product differently, resulting in variable price sensitivity. As a result, you should measure the price sensitivity of each of your market segments separately to ensure that the data you acquire is representative.

Following segmentation of your target market, adopt a process that goes beyond merely asking people, "How much would you pay for product X?"Because it is very impossible for people to precisely estimate their willingness to pay cognitively, researchers have devised strategies to overcome this mental barrier.

1. Price ladder technique

Price laddering is asking potential buyers if they intend to buy a specific product at a specific price, which is commonly ranked on a scale of 1 to 10. If the respondent's intention to purchase an answer is less than a certain threshold (typically 8), the price is low, and they are asked if they want to purchase again. This process might theoretically go on indefinitely, but to minimize undue response bias, respondents are only questioned about a maximum of three different price points. The data is then analyzed to determine the percentage of the market that would buy at any given price.

2. Van Westendorp Technique

By polling respondents on their willingness to pay in ranges, the Van Westendorp question overcomes the difficulty of evaluating price sensitivity. Four questions are asked to each consumer: At what price would you consider the product to be "too low"priced, implying that the quality might be subpar? At what point do you consider the product to be sufficiently expensive that it is not out of the question, but you would have to think twice before purchasing it? At what price do you consider the product to be a steal, a good value for the money? The first two questions require responders to anchor to a reasonable price range, while the latter two questions assist in narrowing down an optimal price range. You can plot the responses and identify a more exact optimal price point once a statistically significant number of people react.

In estimating the price sensitivity of relatively new products, the Van Westendorp question provides a clear efficiency gain. It will also provide extra information regarding the price sensitivity of your product, which will expedite the data collection process. The Van Westendorp Price Sensitivity Meter has helped hundreds of brands over the years. It can help you determine price sensitivity by indicating how much different segments of your target customers are willing to pay for your products. To better visualize the results, use the Van Westendorp price sensitivity question in Question Pro and plot the answers in real-time. The price sensitivity meter is also the only tool that considers low price points to the point when customers begin to question the product's quality. This makes Van Westendorp's results far more comprehensive than those derived using the price scale.

3 Gabor-Granger Pricing Method

The Gabor-Granger pricing approach is a convenient and practical pricing research tool for determining an acceptable price for a given product or service.

After introducing the product, respondents are exposed to a randomly selected price from a predefined pricing list. The respondent is asked if he or she is willing to buy the goods or service at the provided price. If the respondent is willing to purchase the product at that price, the product is displayed again, but this time with a higher price from the predetermined price list.

If the respondent is unable to obtain the goods at the primary price displayed, the merchandise is displayed again at a reduced cost from a predetermined list. This practice is repeated several times until the maximum price a respondent is willing to pay is determined.

Differences between Gabor-Granger and Van Westendorp pricing sensitivity models

For already existing products, the Gabor-Granger model is the most commonly used price sensitivity model. This model provides a price estimate for willingness to pay for your product or service that is directionally right. It gives the revenue optimum price point, demand curve, and price elasticity, which assists researchers in correctly pricing a product. This strategy is only beneficial when you want to look at your brand without taking into account the competitors. This model is limited to preset pricing points.

The Van Westendorp price sensitivity model is the most commonly utilized for new product pricing. When you're not sure what price points the market will tolerate, use Van Westendorp. This model operates across the entire cost spectrum. It will offer users a reasonable pricing range. It will aid in comprehending the respondents' sentiments toward a product or service.

The Benefits and Drawbacks of the Gabor Granger Pricing Technique

The Gabor-Granger approach requires little survey labor and is simple to construct and implement. This pricing technique provides critical information about how much a buyer is willing to pay for a product as well as the perceived value by respondents. As a result, it has become an essential tool in pricing analytics. One clear disadvantage of the Gabor-Granger technique is that competitive products are disregarded throughout the study phase. This means that if a competitor delivers a similar product at a lower price, the price point in your research renders your study worthless. Because of the aforementioned misconception, research is rendered ineffective because they lack context regarding market realities.

To counteract a negative impact on the pricing study, displaying a shelf with rivals' products and prices allows respondents to compare price points.According to studies, when competitors' items and pricing are displayed upfront,

Gabor-Granger results are significantly closer to reality.

The Gabor-Granger approach is especially useful in the following situations: The organization has a predetermined range of acceptable likely prices for the product or service. The offering is so fresh that there are no comparable items or competitors in the market, and the respondents have no prior experience with a product with a similar style and features. The Gabor Granger price modeling technique is demonstrated and applied in this case study.

How do you calculate price sensitivity?
Price sensitivity is calculated by dividing the percentage change in quantity needed by the price change.

formula for price sensitivity

To demonstrate price sensitivity, suppose that when apple nectar costs in a local plant rise by 60%, juice purchases reduce by 25%. We can easily compute the price sensitivity of apple nectar using the algorithm above. -25% sensitivity / 60% sensitivity = -0.42.

As a result, we may conclude that every percentage rise in the price of apple nectar influences the purchase by nearly half of that percentage. Similarly, all items can be evaluated in terms of price changes as well as increases or decreases in demand. Those products are deemed price sensitive when the price change is minor but has a substantial impact on demand. This is frequently the case with convenience items or items with numerous alternatives. Price inelastic products are those that are not extremely responsive to price changes. Such items are typically items of everyday use, and most consumers have no choice but to purchase them.

Sales Channel

A sales channel is any of the different methods or channels that a firm uses to offer its products or services to clients. Direct sales, such as those made through a company's website or physical store, can be made through these channels, as can indirect sales made through third-party intermediaries such as wholesalers, retailers, distributors, or online marketplaces. Online sales, telemarketing, and partnerships with other firms are all examples of sales channels. The selection of sales channels can have a considerable impact on a company's distribution strategy and ability to reach its target audience.

Businesses should select their sales channel and sales channel marketing tactics based on the type of products they sell, their target demographic, competitor activity, and available resources.Some businesses will just employ one sales channel, especially if they have a small product line and a limited budget.Larger companies often employ multiple channels to contact as many potential clients as possible. You might sell all of your products through all channels, or you might simply sell some items through one.

There are several sorts of sales channels, including:

1. Direct Sales: Selling items or services directly to clients without the use of intermediaries. Selling using a company's own website, physical stores, or sales reps are some examples.

2. Retail Sales: Businesses can distribute their products through traditional brick-and-mortar retail outlets, either owned and run by the company or in collaboration with existing merchants.

3. Wholesale: Companies can sell their items in bulk to wholesalers, who then resell them to retailers. Wholesalers frequently purchase in huge numbers and provide products at reduced costs to retailers.

4. Distributor Sales: Businesses can engage with distributors that buy in bulk and then sell and distribute their items to various retailers or end customers in certain regions or marketplaces.

5. Online Marketplaces: Many businesses offer their items on popular e-commerce sites like Amazon, eBay, or Alibaba to reach a larger online customer base.

6. Telemarketing: This is the practice of selling goods or services over the phone. Telemarketers perform outbound sales calls to potential customers.

7. Affiliate Marketing: Businesses can collaborate with individuals or other businesses (affiliates) to market their products in exchange for a commission on each transaction.

8. Social Media Sales: Using social media channels like Instagram, Facebook, or Pinterest to exhibit and sell products to customers directly.

9. Partnerships and Reseller Agreements: Working with other companies or resellers to market and sell your products as part of their services.

10. Direct Mail: Sending marketing materials and catalogs to potential clients via postal mail in order to encourage them to make a purchase.

The selection of sales channels is influenced by factors such as target audience, product or service nature, company resources, and overall business strategy. Companies frequently combine various sales channels to increase their reach and sales potential.

The Significance of Sales Channel

Sales channels assist you in getting your products in front of those who want to buy them. By establishing the proper channels for your company, you can develop a streamlined procedure for marketing and selling your items, thereby increasing the efficiency of your sales force. It is critical to comprehend how various sales channels might benefit your firm. Because of digital technology, there are considerably more channels to pick from than there were previously. You must keep an eye on these to ensure they are working properly. Your marketing efforts are also influenced by the channels you use. When you start selling online, for example, you'll need different eCommerce marketing strategies than when you sell in-store.

Sales Channel Strategy Types

There are three major types of sales channel strategies that influence how you sell items and/or services. The best one for you will be determined by your business model and available resources.

Direct selling

The buyer purchases the product directly from your firm with direct sales. They may do so online or through a mail-order catalog, or you may sell in person through classic door-to-door sales or trade fair presentations. Whatever strategy you pick, PandaDoc can assist your sales people in this area as well. The user-friendly editor, for example, makes it quick and easy to produce selling sheets that will wow leads and prospects. Direct sales do not involve putting goods into retail storefronts or marketplaces like Amazon, whether you are the maker of the goods or have purchased them from another company to sell. Essentially, you are eliminating the middleman.

This strategy keeps all parts of order fulfillment in-house, necessitating additional effort and resources. Warehouses, logistical systems, trucks, and delivery personnel are often required. The benefits include maintaining control over your operations and a direct connection with customers, as well as avoiding the costs associated with third-party selling.

Sales through intermediaries

Indirect sales are when you sell your products and services to customers via third-party intermediaries such as retailers, wholesalers, dealerships, or other intermediaries.Because they already have a client base and the infrastructure for enhanced fulfillment, these distribution channels help you reach a larger audience. If you don't have your own resources, this is a decent option. The disadvantage is that you will lose control and would have to pay these intermediaries to sell on your behalf.You could use sales agents or resellers in addition to distributors. Sales agents agree to sell a company's products in exchange for a fee, whereas resellers buy products (typically in bulk and at a discount) and resell them profitably. Meanwhile, with white-label sales, you sell your products to another company, which then labels the product before selling it to the ultimate client.

Consumer purchases

Companies that use multichannel marketing (discussed later) can sell through both direct and indirect channels. They'll employ catalogs and email campaigns to sell directly to consumers and maintain a personal touch, while also selling through online marketplaces or retail chains to reach a larger audience. Consider Amazon. It sells things directly to consumers, but customers can also buy products from independent businesses on Amazon's site. These retailers are then in charge of fulfilling orders.

How to Develop a Successful Deals Channel Strategy

Whether you are sticking with many channels to grow your business or planning to expand into multiple new areas, you need a solid strategy in place. produce a business plan that addresses all of your pretensions, and be prepared to acclimatize as request trends and customer actions shift. Here are some pointers for developing an effective sales channel strategy:

1. Consider the goods or services

It is critical to thoroughly consider the items or services you sell, as well as the best channel for marketing them. Begin by producing a report that includes each product category, its price point, sales costs, and revenue from existing channels. You'll need a solid understanding of your present and prospective clients, so look at past data and market trends. Where do people like to purchase your products? Why not conduct a poll and ask them? Do you sell products aimed at a specific demographic or segment? Electronic signature software, for example, is frequently offered to people who deal with legal transactions, so you definitely wouldn't promote it on a young network like TikTok.

2. Select the appropriate channel

You may now utilize all of that information to select the best channel. Assume you're selling a fun product aimed toward teenagers. In this instance, you may leverage influencer marketing. Alternatively, if a large number of people are connecting with your Instagram posts, you might begin selling on the site using direct purchasing solutions. It all comes down to how many individuals you can reach through each sales channel and how well they match your target market. As previously said, your budget is an important consideration, as you will require the necessary resources to set up and manage new channels.

3. Look for dependable partners

Business partnerships can be an effective method to pool resources and broaden your reach. Affiliate marketers and influencers, for example, already have an audience, whereas online marketplaces will handle at least part of the sales process for you. You might also collaborate with other companies to cross-promote one other's products, especially if they have strong marketing plans in place. Don't forget about your shipping partners and suppliers—you'll need strong ties with them to handle all of those extra orders. It's critical that your partners are trustworthy, so do your homework before entering into any kind of relationship.

4. Establish limits

When working with partners, you must establish expectations for how the partnership will function. For example, what type of sales increase do you anticipate from your affiliates, and when will they be paid? How will the shipping process function, and who will be held accountable if something goes wrong? You may also collaborate with internal partners, such as your company's marketing or product development teams. In either case, it's best to get everything in writing with a contract. In addition, you should create some standards for managing your sales channels, detailing things like the maximum desired response time for client queries and your return policy.

5. Monitor sales channels

It's critical to monitor the performance of all your sales channels; otherwise, you won't know which ones are the most effective. You'll need tools to assist you, such as a sales management platform that allows you to view sales and revenue in one spot. Monitor the outcomes of your partners as well. Use these indicators to build frequent reports that account for external factors like seasonality, and look into what you can do to shorten a long sales cycle. Sending satisfaction questionnaires to your clients will help you identify any problems. That way, you'll know when to change your strategy.

CHAPTER 4: Exploring your Marketing Objectives

Every successful business usually has a marketing plan with minor goals that support it. It is critical to have these goals in place so that everyone in marketing or within the organization can work together toward a common goal. Objectives let you determine whether your efforts were effective or not, and what you should reconsider before initiating a new campaign.

Marketing objectives are made up of smaller and shorter-term activities that a marketing representative or department must do in order to achieve the longer-term and overarching marketing goals. Marketing objectives are distinct from marketing goals, however the terms are sometimes used interchangeably. Marketing objectives are often short-term and specific, with timelines, measurement methods, and other factors used to develop them. Marketing objectives are more long-term and align with a company's overall mission and purpose. You employ your marketing aims to achieve your marketing objectives.

Using the SMART technique of goal generation, you can create marketing objectives. This will guarantee that the objectives established provide direction to all involved in marketing, establish clear advice when deciding on campaigns and how best to reach your target demographic, and describe the actual purpose of the marketing team.

SMART objectives are as follows: Marketing goals that are clear enable for more successful preparation.

- Measurable: You must be able to track your progress toward your goal. If you can't measure the impact of your plan on your aim, you should probably rethink your goal or set a more specific one.

- Achievable: Think about goals that you and your team can attain in a reasonable amount of time. It should be extremely possible to see this goal realized.

- Relevance: It is also critical to ensure that the marketing objectives are relevant.

They should include previously established aims and values and explain what the organization stands for as a whole.

- Time-based goals should have an end date set for when you wish to achieve the goal. Timeframes keep people engaged, and if you don't accomplish your goals within the timeframe, you'll be able to understand why and pivot more effectively.

How do you Set Marketing Goals

Creating a marketing proposal is a simple process, but it should not be rushed. You must involve everyone and develop measurable marketing objectives that align with your organization's vision. Let's take a look at the following steps:

Step 1: Examine your organization's aims

Every goal, marketing or otherwise, must contribute to your broader business goals. Read over your company's vision and strategy and brainstorm steps that would bring you one step closer to attaining the dream that your strategy outlines. If the goal does not propel you in that direction, it is a distraction and should be ignored.

Tip: If you're having difficulty identifying organizational goals, it may be an indication that you need to go back a step further and create a definite and clear vision for the company.

Step 2: Collaborate with the team to brainstorm

It is critical not to try to do everything on your own. Set up a meeting with your marketing team to work through these issues. Request that everyone prepare for the meeting by developing some of their own objectives, and then walk around the room to discuss them and determine what marketing collateral will be required to complete the job.

Tip: Involve your sales team as well, because they can tell you what kind of marketing output will help them close more business.

Step 3: Establish the goals

After everyone has given their input, create an initial list of objectives and schedule a follow-up meeting to go over them. Here you can discuss these goals in greater depth, such as if the time limit is reasonable or whether the proper individuals are assigned to the right responsibilities.

Tip: Keep in mind that these goals must be specific and measurable. Consider how you would demonstrate that we met this goal. If you can't express what success looks like, you'll need to do extra work to define the goal.

Step 4: Create a marketing strategy

Now that you've established your marketing objectives, it's time to create a marketing strategy to support them. Make a step-by-step plan outlining how you will attain each goal and in what time period. It should also specify who the stakeholders are and who is responsible for what.

Tip: Being explicit when setting marketing objectives will assist you in identifying clear next steps. Break down the steps as much as possible to develop simple activities that the team can perform to maximize the likelihood of success.

Step 5: Assess the outcomes and then regroup
Consider the objectives as a cycle rather than a journey to a destination. After you've done steps 1-4, you should assess your performance on a regular basis, possibly quarterly, and then meet to discuss it. What went well? What didn't work?

Did we meet our marketing objectives? What should we change in the coming quarter? Use tools to track key marketing indicators like leads and website traffic. Many software choices can generate extensive reports that might assist you in identifying trends or flaws.

Why are Marketing Objectives so Important?

Your marketing objectives will lack clarity and follow-through if they are not defined.Marketing goals are important for various reasons:

1. Focus and Direction: They provide your marketing activities a clear sense of purpose and direction. Without objectives, your marketing campaigns risk becoming aimless.

2. Measurability: Objectives function as measurable targets. They enable you to monitor and evaluate the success of your marketing campaigns. This data-driven strategy facilitates making sound decisions.

3. Alignment: They aid in the alignment of marketing efforts with overall business objectives. When your marketing goals align with those of your firm, you're more likely to make a significant contribution to the bottom line.

4. Resource Allocation: Goals help with resource allocation. Budget, time, and manpower can be allocated based on the importance of each aim.

5. Motivation: Setting specific marketing goals will help encourage your staff. When goals are completed, it provides them a sense of purpose and accomplishment.

6. Adaptability: Setting goals allows you to modify and adjust your marketing techniques if you aren't meeting them. It serves as a foundation for learning and improvement.

7. Communication: It improves communication inside the marketing team as well as with other departments. Everyone is aware of what is being worked on and why.

8. Strategy Development: Your marketing strategy is built on the foundation of your marketing objectives. They assist you in defining the "what"and "why"of your marketing initiatives, which in turn influences the "how."Your approach may become disorganized and ineffectual if you do not have defined objectives.

9. Market Segmentation and Targeting: Marketing objectives aid in establishing your target audience and market segmentation. By defining your objectives, you can personalize your messaging and campaigns to efficiently reach the proper people.

10. Competitive Advantage: Marketing objectives that are well-defined might help you acquire a competitive advantage. They enable you to detect market gaps and create distinctive selling propositions that resonate with your target audience.

11. Budget Control: Setting goals is critical for budget planning. You may direct resources to where they are most needed, ensuring that your budget is spent wisely to achieve your objectives.

12. Risk Management: Risk assessment is also influenced by objectives. They assist you in anticipating potential issues and developing risk-mitigation strategies to keep your marketing activities on track.

13. Customer Engagement: Customer engagement goals, such as promoting customer loyalty or advocacy, are frequently included in marketing objectives. This emphasis on the customer experience has the potential to lead to long-term connections and repeat business.

14. Feedback and Learning: When you have certain goals in mind, you can collect data and feedback to assess your performance. This feedback loop allows you to continuously learn and improve your marketing efforts.

15. Long-term Planning: Marketing aims aren't simply about making money in the short term. They should include both short-term and long-term objectives, allowing you to plan for long-term growth while also adapting to market changes.

16. Accountability: Goals create accountability within your marketing team. Team members can take responsibility for specific goals, and progress can be tracked and assessed on a regular basis.

In summary, marketing objectives are an essential component of efficient marketing strategy, giving direction, measurement, and a mechanism to tie marketing efforts to broader corporate objectives. They direct your actions, assist you in adapting to an ever-changing market, and guarantee that your marketing efforts are in line with your company's overall goals.

CHAPTER 5: Exploring Advertising and Collaborating with Agencies

Advertising is a marketing strategy that involves paying for advertising space to promote a product, service, or beget. announcements, or advertisements for short, are the real marketable messaging. Advertising's purpose is to communicate those who are most likely to be willing to pay for a company's products or services and convert them to buy. Companies can use advertising to get their products and services in front of the public. Advertising media ranges from fliers and business cards to online display and print advertisements on broadcast television and radio. Advertising moment interacts with its followership via online platforms similar as LinkedIn, Facebook, Instagram, Pinterest, and YouTube.

Advertising reaches a large number of people with the primary goal of Creating profit for businesses of all sizes. adding brand mindfulness to ensure that products remain in consumers' minds. prevailing people to support the operations of nonprofits, governmental and non-governmental associations, political parties, religious confederations, and other associations. Advertising is one of several sub-disciplines within the larger discipline of marketing. hype and public relations, branding, telemarketing, client relations, and direct marketing are some of the other crucial subdisciplines. While advertising ways are more broad- grounded and can be regarded as a scattershot strategy to landing consumers' attention, marketing strategies are more focused. It focuses on demographics similar to gender, age, occupation, terrain, interests and pursuits, pretensions(similar as first- time home purchasers and unborn council scholars) and life- changing events(similar as marriage, withdrawal, and parenthood). Advertising is an important expenditure for any establishment, anyhow of size.

What's the Significance of Advertising: 7 major advantages announcement

Juggernauts can help you reach further from the right people, whether you are introducing a new product or service or simply seeking to get your brand out there. Then there are seven important ways an advertising strategy can make your company flourish.

1. Raising mindfulness Increased mindfulness of your brand, product, or service is one of the most direct goods of advertising. Your target guests will most probably need to see your business many times before they flash back to you, and marketing juggernauts can help you achieve this. Marketers constantly use paid announcements to not only ameliorate exposure but also to constantly reach the same consumers. numerous

internet platforms use trackers known as"eyefuls"to discover who has viewed your announcement preliminarily. Businesses like yours can use this data to retarget the same callers through digital advertising. With this harmonious reach, you can establish a strong presence in your target request.

2. Educating guests Advertising informs people about how your products or services can profit them and what your brand stands for. announcement juggernauts can help you establish your brand and induce a deeper understanding of it, from your company's ideal to the value of what you sell. Your target request will have a lesser connection to your brand as they learn further about your company, which will help you establish consumer trust and fidelity and move you one step closer to

generating a trade. announcement juggernauts can also be used to educate people on themes important to your business. A plumber marketing crusade, for illustration, might run a social media announcement with an infographic describing an easy trick to fix a restroom clog. You may boost your visibility as an assistant expert while also encouraging people to discover further about your company by doing so.

3. Ameliorate your character Advertising allows you to ameliorate the character of your small business. Offline and online advertising may both increase the visibility of your main dispatches and the takeaways you want your target followership to have — and promote your company's stylish rates. You can shape customer comprehension (also known as your brand image) by using announcements to evoke

specific feelings or to explain the story behind your brand. For illustration, if you've had any unfavorable exposure, airing an ad that shows the positive aspects of your company can divert potential customers away from the negative attention.

4. Obtain new customers

Acquiring new clients is essential for business expansion. Online advertising, such as social media ads, Yelp ads, search engine ads, and others, is especially important for consumer acquisition. You don't have to appeal to a wide audience with web commercials, as you would with traditional advertising channels like print ads or television. You can reach out to people who fit your target demographics and key interests with digital media advertising.

Reaching your exact target market means you won't waste money advertising to people your firm doesn't serve, which increases your return on investment (ROI). In the case of Yelp Ads, you will only be charged when a user clicks on your ad, whereas impressions are free (when people see your ad but do not click). This means that your advertising dollars are directed solely toward appealing to your target audience. As a result, advertising can be one of the most cost-effective methods of generating leads and converting new clients to your business. For example, if you own a luxury automobile repair shop, you might utilize digital advertising to precisely target high-income citizens in your neighborhood rather than advertising on a billboard or in a magazine to a larger audience that may or may not be interested in your services.

5. Retain current customers

Customer retention is the bedrock of corporate expansion. You need returning customers that adore your brand, offer you referrals, and are inclined to spend more money on your product or service when completely engaged. As a result, you can employ ad campaigns to retarget people of your target audience, including existing customers. Reminding clients of your brand on a regular basis, possibly by giving new products or discounted pricing for loyal members, encourages them to feel connected to you and buy from your company rather than competitors.

The greater your brand loyalty, the less you will need to invest in marketing to generate a sale. Because engaged customers are 23% more likely to spend than dissatisfied customers, selling to existing customers can be far easier and less expensive than investing substantial time in developing relationships with prospects who may never become customers.

6. Maintain a competitive advantage.

You have challengers no matter what type of business you run. There will always be brands contending for the same consumers' attention. Indeed if you do not know who your challengers are, chances are they are one of the innumerous brands that contribute to the billion-bone advertising assiduity. The significance of advertising stems from the fact that everyone is doing it. However, your challengers will reluctantly seize the limelight, If you don't use announcements to keep your brand in front of people's minds. And if you remain in the murk for too long, you'll lose significance in the minds of consumers.

Staying ahead of the competition, especially in crowded diligence, requires constant exposure. Advertisements can help you achieve this in addition to the organic(free) or word- of- mouth reach you formerly have. Yelp Advertisements, for illustration, allows your business to show above hunt results for applicable terms as well as on challengers' runners. You also have the capability to change your budget at any time, icing that you optimize exposure while Norway is overspending.

7. Increase your deals. People in a deals meeting In response to the question,"Why is advertising important?""It's critical to mention its impact on deals."Advertisements are effective tools for

aiding small businesses in earning the finances they bear to survive and develop. Still, announcement juggernauts can directly enhance deals by attracting further guests to your physical store, website, If you enjoy an online brand. On average, digital hunt advertisements help businesses earn$ 11 for every bone invested.

Traditional or digital advertising can also help you boost the value of consumer purchases by cross-selling or recommending reciprocal particulars and services. A hair salon, for illustration, could sell its blow dry, styling, and coloring services in addition to haircuts. The further guests are apprehensive of your goods and services and how they may benefit from them — the more likely it's that they will acquire fresh goods and services in addition to their original purchase. Meet your business objects. Advertising is pivotal since it can help a company develop.

Advertising can help you reach the correct followership with positive, targeted communication that transforms implicit guests into paying guests and boost your small company selling sweats. It also assists you in retargeting your followership, whether you want to increase brand mindfulness or promote reprise business from pious guests.

Advertising Types

Advertising media exemplifications include Websites and social media are exemplifications of digital platforms. Television, radio, print (for example, in specialized journals read by your target demographic), cinema marketing, billboards and bus shelters, Door-to-door selling. Finding the ideal advertising mix for your company might be difficult with so many options. The type of advertising you choose should be determined by:

- your company
- your financial situation

Social media, for example, may be a free or low-cost option to advertise, but it is used differently by different age groups. Make certain that your target audience has access to your advertising platform. Using a variety of media may be advantageous.

Partnering with Agencies

Collaborating with advertising agencies is collaborating with external organizations or corporations that specialize in various parts of advertising and marketing to assist in the planning, creation, and execution of your advertising campaigns. Collaboration with advertising agency entails the following:

1. Creative Services: Agencies can assist in the development of creative concepts, the design of commercials, and the creation of captivating content that resonates with your target audience.

2. Advertising firms have teams of people who are experts in many areas of advertising, such as creative design, copywriting, media buying, and digital marketing. You obtain access to their

specific expertise and abilities by partnering with them.

3. Media Planning and Buying: Agencies can help you choose the best advertising channels and media platforms to reach your target audience. They are capable of negotiating media placements and optimizing ad budgets.

4. Strategic Planning: Agencies can assist you in developing a strategic advertising plan that is in line with your company's aims and target market. They frequently perform market research and analysis to help guide their strategies.

5. Campaign Execution: Advertising firms handle all parts of campaign execution, from ad content creation to campaign launch and monitoring.

6. Tracking and analytics: Agencies frequently offer thorough data analysis and reporting to help you analyze the success of your advertising efforts and make required changes.

7. Collaboration with agencies can help you save time and resources, allowing you to focus on your main business activities.

8. Scalability: Agencies can scale to meet your advertising needs, whether they are one-time or continuous.

9. Define Clear Objectives: Before approaching an agency, you should have a firm grasp on your advertising goals and objectives. Whether it's brand exposure, lead generation, revenue, or another goal, outlining it will help the agency develop effective methods.

10. Considerations for Budget: Create a reasonable budget for your advertising initiatives. Inform the agency about your financial limits so that they can adapt their advice properly.

11. Research and Selection: When choosing an agency, do your homework. Seek out agencies who have a proven track record in your sector or area. To evaluate their prior performance, request case studies and client references.

12. Collaboration requires open and effective communication. Communicate your brand's identity, values, and messaging to the agency in

a clear and consistent manner throughout the campaign.

13. Project timetables: Agree on project timetables and milestones so that everyone is on the same page when it comes to campaign start dates, reviews, and reporting schedules.

14. Guidance vs. Creative Freedom: Strike a balance between creative freedom and particular guidance. While agencies are experts, your feedback as a client is important, so strike a balance that allows for creative cooperation.

15. Metrics and key performance indicators (KPIs): Determine the key performance indicators (KPIs) that will be used to assess campaign success. Agencies should be ready to explain how they plan to track and report on these metrics.

16. Legal and contractual agreements: In a formal contract, clearly explain the parameters of your relationship. This should include the scope of the project, payment terms, confidentiality, and any other legal considerations.

17. Set up frequent performance evaluations to measure the impact of campaigns and discuss any necessary improvements.

18. Flexibility: Be willing to change strategies based on campaign results and changing market conditions. A competent firm will be responsive and adaptable when it comes to campaign optimization.

Keep in mind that working with an agency is a partnership. When both sides collaborate well, it can result in successful advertising campaigns that advance your company's goals. It is critical to select the ideal agency that fits your brand, goals, and budget while also communicating successfully with your team. Collaboration with an agency can improve the effectiveness of your advertising efforts.

When is it best to Advertise?

The best time to advertise a product is determined by a number of factors, including your target audience, the nature of the product, and your marketing objectives. However, some general temporal considerations include:

1. Seasonality: Market products that correspond to the seasons or holidays, like summer clothing in the spring or holiday gifts in the winter.

2. Product Launch: Create excitement and expectation by advertising when releasing a new product.

3. Trends and Events: Capitalize on trending topics or events that are relevant to your product.

4. Sales Cycles: Align your advertising with the sales cycles of your sector, such as back-to-school promotions or Black Friday offers.

5. Audience Behavior: Examine your target audience's online activity to see when they're most active and likely to respond to your adverts.

6. Budget and Resources: Consider your advertising campaign budget and resources.

7. A/B Testing: Experiment with different times and analyze the results to find the best timing.

8. Weekday: Some firms discover that certain days of the week are more beneficial for advertising. For example, if you own a restaurant, you may want to advertise on Fridays and weekends when people are making dinner reservations.

9. Consider the time of day when your target audience is most engaged. Morning, noon, and nighttime participation levels might all vary.

10. Local Time Zones: If your audience is scattered over multiple time zones, schedule your adverts to reach them at a time that is convenient for them.

11. Competitor Activity: Pay attention to when your competitors advertise. To stand out or compete more successfully, you may opt to promote at different times.

12. Content Relevance: Make sure that your ad content is timely. Promoting a breakfast offer in the evening, for example, may not be as beneficial as doing so in the morning.

13. Analytics and testing: Constantly monitor and analyze the performance of your adverts. Make data-driven decisions by using analytics to discover when your advertising is most effective.

14. Events and Holidays: Align your advertising with key events, holidays, or special occasions for your target demographic. Promote gift ideas for Mother's Day or Valentine's Day, for example.

15. money Allocation: Distribute your advertising money intelligently throughout the year, focusing on the most essential moments for your company.

16. Evergreen vs. Seasonal Campaigns: Distinguish between evergreen campaigns that run continuously and seasonal campaigns that are created for specific times of the year. This allows for a good mix of consistent brand visibility and timely promotions.

17. Audience Segmentation: If you have a diverse audience, segment them based on their tastes and behaviors, and then plan advertising for each segment separately.

18. User Insights and Data: Use user data and insights from your website or social media platforms to learn when your audience is most active and when they convert.

There is no one-size-fits-all answer to when is the optimum time to advertise, and it varies greatly between different firms and industries. To improve your campaigns, continuously analyze and refine your advertising timing based on performance data and changing market conditions.

Remember that having a well-defined target demographic and a cohesive marketing strategy is what leads to effective advertising. Regardless of the season, these are essential for successful product advertisement.

CHAPTER 6: Enhancing Consumer's Lifetime Value

Every consumer adds value to your company. What makes your customers become devoted followers? How long do they remain? Is it possible to improve your profits during the lifespan of a client? Yes, the answer is yes!

What does Customer Lifetime Value mean?

In eCommerce, client Lifetime Value is a marketing metric that shows the total amount spent by a single client on your products or services over the course of their lifetime. So, one of the best strategies to develop your business is to keep your current clients and raise their lifetime value. The longer a happy customer stays with you, the more profit he or she delivers to your company. Customer Lifetime Value (CLV or LTV) is a crucial marketing and business indicator that represents the overall revenue a customer is expected to contribute for a firm over the course of their relationship. It is a method of calculating a customer's long-term value to a company. Here's what CLV is about:

1. Predictive Value: CLV is a forward-looking prediction rather than a historical metric. Based on their previous behavior and interactions with your company, it predicts how much a client will contribute in terms of revenue and profit in the future.

2. Customer Retention: It underlines the need of keeping and nurturing current consumers. A greater CLV frequently indicates that a customer will continue to do business with you in the future.

3. Marketing and Decision-Making: CLV assists organizations in making intelligent marketing budget allocation, client acquisition methods, and pricing decisions. It advises businesses on how much they should spend to gain new customers profitably.

4. Segmentation: It is used to categorize customers based on their worth. Customers with a high CLV are treated differently than those with a low CLV, with more attention and resources spent on retaining and rewarding the former.

5. Customer Satisfaction: A solid customer relationship generally leads in a better CLV. Customers that are pleased with your services are more likely to return and suggest others to you.

6. Calculations: Calculating CLV can be complicated, as it may require taking into account parameters such as average purchase value, buy frequency, customer turnover rate, and expected client longevity.

7. Financial indicator: Customer lifetime value (CLV) is an essential financial indicator that allows organizations to assess the long-term health and growth potential of their customer base.

In conclusion, Customer Lifetime Value is a forward-thinking statistic that assists businesses in understanding the financial value of their customer connections and making strategic decisions to optimize that value over time. It focuses on the significance of client retention, satisfaction, and effective marketing methods.

What does a client lifetime value look like?

For example, suppose a typical restaurant client goes once per month and spends $17 per visit during a 10-year lifetime. The client lifetime value is computed as follows: $17 x 12 x 10 = $2,040.

Why is Lifetime Customer Value Important to your Business

CLV assists you in developing more accurate financial predictions for your company as well as better marketing strategy decisions. It's easier to have clarity about things like your customer acquisition marketing costs when you know how much profit a client will deliver you over its lifespan. It also allows you to understand more clearly if there is anything you can or should do to boost customer relationships with your brand. It is possible to change techniques that drive your firm to boost client lifetime by taking a closer look at factors like average order value and average purchasing frequency and comparing them to past data.

If you're still not convinced, here are a few more reasons why CLV is critical:

Customers who are returning spend more than new customers. According to studies, existing customers spend 67% more than new consumers. Keeping existing customers costs five times less than getting new ones. Acquiring new consumers by reaching out to them, guiding them through a marketing funnel, and onboarding them is expensive, but existing customers have already gone through these steps.

Customers who have previously purchased are more likely to do so again. Selling to a current customer has a probability of 60-70%, while selling to a new customer has a probability of only 5-20%. Furthermore, boosting customer retention by 5% boosts earnings by 25-95%

(read more about increasing retention with cohort analysis here). But the unexpected fact is that around 50% of organizations prefer to put greater focus on their client acquisition approach vs. 18% that focus on retention. Knowing the facts above, we can see that Customer Lifetime Value is an important indicator that is underutilized. That is, however, good news for you! You have an advantage and can remain ahead of some of the competitors by focusing on it.

CLV assists firms in anticipating future income and profitability, allowing them to set attainable financial goals and manage resources wisely. It directs resource allocation, particularly in marketing and client acquisition, by calculating the allowable cost of attracting and retaining customers for long-term profitability. Businesses can segment their client base based on CLV, enabling them to develop specialized strategies that favor high-value customers and improve long-term loyalty.

Understanding CLV enables firms to concentrate on enhancing customer pleasure and loyalty, which leads to long-term profits. Having a high CLV frequently signifies having a competitive advantage in customer retention, as retaining existing customers can be more cost-effective than constantly gaining new ones. CLV influences pricing decisions, ensuring that prices cover costs while maximizing profitability over the lifetime of a customer. It has an impact on product and service development by pushing companies to create offers that cater to the tastes of high-CLV customers. Businesses who understand CLV may enhance their marketing strategy, target the correct demographic, and increase the efficiency of their marketing campaigns.

An emphasis on CLV frequently leads to measures to reduce customer churn, which is critical for retaining valuable customers. Furthermore, a well-thought-out CLV strategy can boost investor and stakeholder confidence by demonstrating a company's ability to plan for long-term sustainability and growth. In essence, CLV is a strategic metric for long-term customer relationship, profitability, and competitive advantage optimization.

How to Increase Customer Loyalty

Focusing on Customer Satisfaction and Customer Retention is the best method to maximize your customers' lifetime value (read more about retention metrics here). Here are five practical methods for achieving and maintaining this goal.

1. Provide a Referral Program

Referral programs are an excellent approach to boost the lifetime value of your customers. Customers who are referred have a 16% greater lifetime value and 18% lower churn (also known as customer attrition). In addition, 81% of consumers trust suggestions from people they know, and 55% discuss their new purchases on social media. This means that by establishing a referral program, you boost your CLV while also gaining exposure to new potential consumers, who can later be converted into loyal customers.

2. Offer targeted and personalized campaigns

Email marketing is the most effective digital marketing approach for customer retention, according to 56% of digital marketers. Many firms, however, fail to produce valuable content. Rather than delivering valuable information, they limit themselves to automated campaigns that provide no real value.

Sending targeted and personalized campaigns allows you to focus on individual clients and engage them with material that is tailored to them.

3. Prioritize them - Listen to your customers

Your business performance will show whether the majority of your clients are satisfied or not. However, in order to effectively estimate their happiness, always acquire the appropriate data. In this scenario, a brief survey is appropriate. You can include the following in there: On a scale of 1 to 10, how likely is it that the customer would refer your items to someone else? Where could things be better (product description, presentation, shipping charges, etc.) A quick comment is optional for any extra feedback. Giving your consumers a method to provide feedback makes them an essential part of your company's progress. Customers will appreciate your efforts and will likely remain loyal to your company if you listen to their opinions and improve when possible.

4. Produce Content to Keep Customers Involved

Content marketing is here to stay, and it may make your customers feel more connected and involved with your business if done correctly. When you create content that focuses on your customers' main pain areas, or on educating and bringing your leads through the sales funnel, you have a far better chance of increasing CLV and lowering customer acquisition costs. Customers that create a relationship with your business will not only be loyal to you for a longer period of time, but will also help promote your brand through their social media platforms or word-of-mouth. When they are your biggest fans, chances are they will buy from you more frequently, and providing information that is valuable to them - whether on your blog, social media, or through e-mail marketing - is a terrific method to do so.

5. Improve Your Customer Service

Better customer service results in a better customer experience, which boosts customer retention and lifetime value. Make sure your company is active on several social media networks, as 66% of customers contact assistance via at least three separate channels. Then, determine which channels your customers prefer and devote resources accordingly. Clients typically demand a quick response to their inquiries, requests, and complaints, thus you should preferably give live chat assistance 24 hours a day, seven days a week. If you don't have the resources to do so, respond to clients as soon as possible because 84% of consumers want a response within 24 hours if they post complaints on social media.

6. Recognize and Reward Your Most Loyal Customers

You may identify which clients are the most devoted to you by estimating the lifetime value of each customer. This is an excellent moment to strengthen your relationships with these consumers by providing them with special incentives. These promotions may include reduced (or free) delivery, first access to new items, and assured order availability for limited and exclusive stock, among other things. Rewarding your most devoted consumers will surely boost their long-term satisfaction and retention.

7. Take Advantage of Cross-Selling and Upselling Strategies

Upselling and cross-selling are two further ways for increasing client lifetime value. The goal here is to provide better solutions to your consumers while boosting their average order value or frequency of purchase. You boost your chances of increasing revenue by providing clients a complimentary product or service to the one they are currently exploring or by presenting them with a superior option with a higher price and more benefits. These are excellent tactics employed by a number of web firms and are well worth attempting. You may also use tactics such as contextual targeting to ensure that your clients see the relevant advertising at the right time.

CONCLUSION

This book takes us on a full journey to develop a successful business strategy. We begin by discussing the significance of this initiative. In Chapter 1, we lead you through the critical early steps, emphasizing the selection of your target market and the formulation of a captivating message to reach your audience effectively. The second chapter delves into providing extraordinary service, creating exceptional products, and sculpting your brand's identity and personality to stand out in the market. Chapter 3 is all about resolving pricing sensitivity and choosing the best sales channels for your items or services. In Chapter 4, we look at the importance of defining clear marketing objectives and why they are so important in attaining your business objectives. Chapter 5 discusses advertising and the significance of cooperating with agencies, as well as the proper timing for advertising efforts. In the last chapter, we underline the vital function of increasing Customer Lifetime Value (CLV) and why it is critical to your company's long-term success.

We share insights, tactics, and actionable recommendations throughout this book to help you develop a strong foundation for your organization and survive in a competitive market.

REVIEW PAGE

Dear Reader,

I sincerely hope this writing meets you well. I am enthusiastically contacting you with a modest request. I just released "Learning the Business Way" and I greatly appreciate your viewpoint. Your knowledge in this field makes your insights extremely valuable.

I genuinely appreciate your attention, and I am aware of how valuable your time is. Your ideas would be very helpful if you could take a moment to read Learning the Business Way.

I appreciate your consideration of my plea. If you require any extra information, I will be pleased to supply it.

Warm regards

Francis A. Wiles